My Pals are Here!

Science
Workbook
5B

Joe · Zoe · Sue

Written by:

Teo-Gwan Wai Lan • Dr Kwa Siew Hwa

mc **Marshall Cavendish**
Education

© 2003 Times Media Private Limited
© 2003 Marshall Cavendish International (Singapore) Private Limited

Published by Marshall Cavendish Education
A member of Times Publishing Limited
Times Centre, 1 New Industrial Road, Singapore 536196
Customer Service Hotline: (65) 6411 0820
E-mail: tmesales@sg.marshallcavendish.com
Website: www.marshallcavendish.com/education/sg

First published 2003
Reprinted 2003, 2004
Second impression 2004
Reprinted 2005, 2006, 2008

ISBN 978-981-01-8371-4

Edited by: Jessie Lau

Printed in Singapore by C.O.S. Printers Pte Ltd

My Pals are Here! **Science** Workbook allows pupils to apply the knowledge that they have learnt in the classroom. It is in line with the latest revised Science syllabus and infuses the Ministry of Education's initiative of thinking skills.

For every chapter in the Textbook, there are corresponding worksheets in this Workbook. The questions in each worksheet are graded so that pupils progress from simple to difficult problems. At the end of a series of worksheets, there are revision worksheets which comprise multiple-choice questions to help pupils revise the concepts.

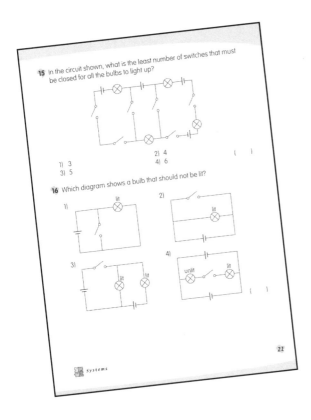

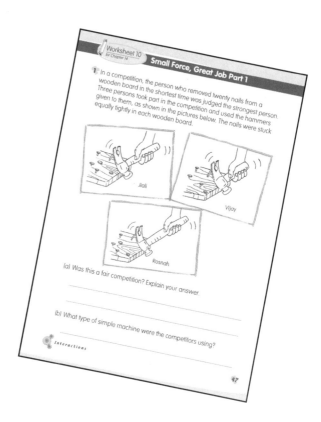

My Pals are Here! **Science** Workbook is designed to give pupils ample practice in exam-oriented questions. It is a self-contained, structured revision programme that prepares them for continual assessments and exams. Pupils will develop confidence to handle more challenging problems upon completion of the worksheets.

C O N T E N T S

1 Some of the items shown below have an electrical system and some do not. Classify them in the table provided on page 2.

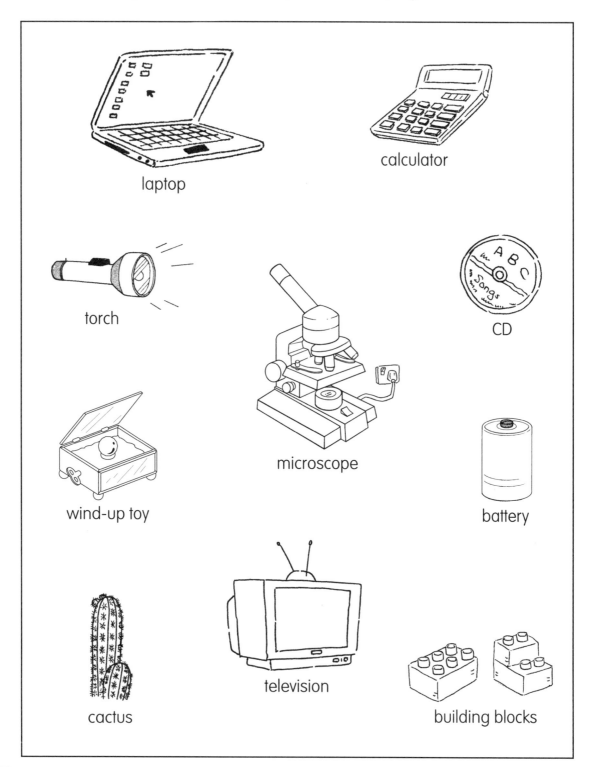

laptop

calculator

torch

microscope

CD

wind-up toy

battery

cactus

television

building blocks

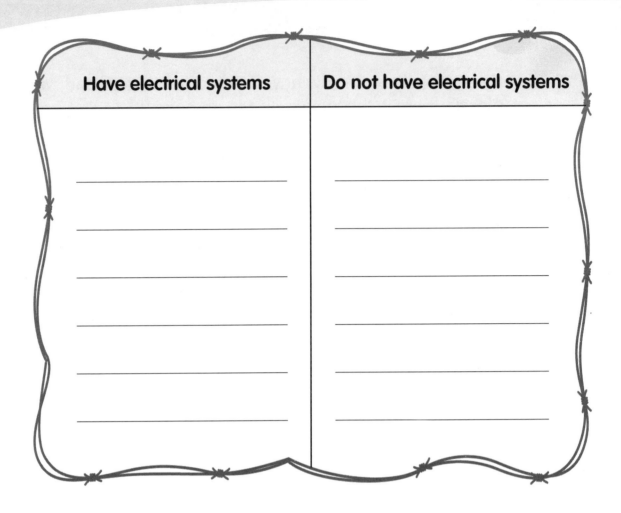

Have electrical systems	Do not have electrical systems
_____	_____
_____	_____
_____	_____
_____	_____
_____	_____
_____	_____

2 The electrical components, A , B and C are shown below.

A

switch

B

bulb in bulb holder

C

battery in
battery holder

Systems

Which component can be connected to each of the following circuits to complete the action stated? In the box provided, write the letter that represents the component.

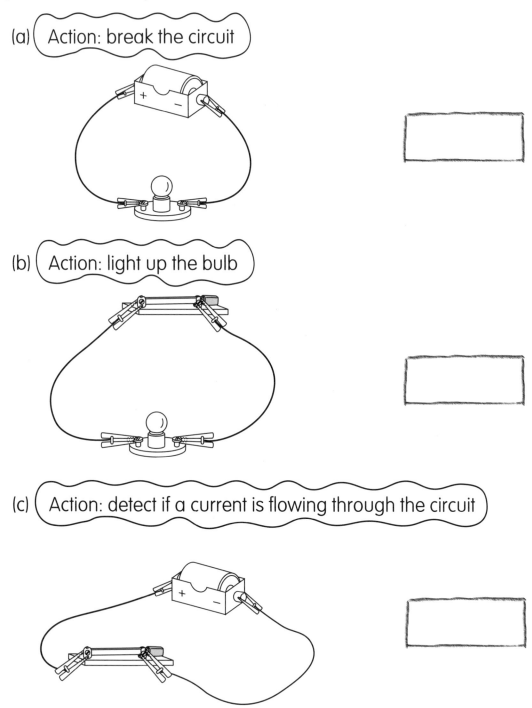

(a) Action: break the circuit

(b) Action: light up the bulb

(c) Action: detect if a current is flowing through the circuit

3 (a) Unscramble the letters to form the correct word for each blank. There is an extra letter that will not be used for each blank.

For a bulb in an electric circuit to function, an electric

_____ c r u s e r n t must

transport _____ g r y e e n y

from the battery to the bulb. This can only happen when

the circuit is _____ s c o l e d s

When the battery and the bulb are connected properly with

_____ s t i w e r , the bulb

_____ s h i l g e t up and

gives off _____ t h a m e .

(b) Write the extra letters in the order that you found them in 3(a) to fill in the blank below.

An electrical _____ can be made up of one or many electric circuits.

4 (a) Look at the circuit shown below. State two ways to make the bulb stop glowing. Explain how they stop the bulb from glowing.

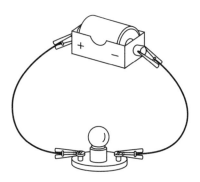

(i) _____

_____

_____

(ii) _____

_____

_____

(b) What electrical component can be connected to the circuit in 4(a) to control the flow of electric current?

_____

5 Use an orange colour pencil to trace the paths that represent closed circuits in the following diagrams.

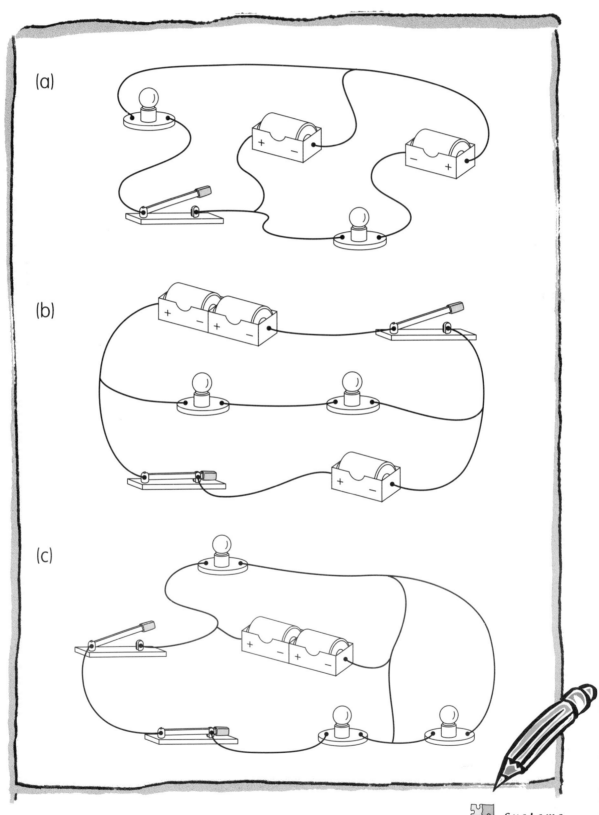

(a)

(b)

(c)

Systems

6 Lee Lee conducted an experiment with the circuit card and the circuit tester shown below. The circuit card had some paper clips clipped onto it. Some of the paper clips were connected by electrical wires.

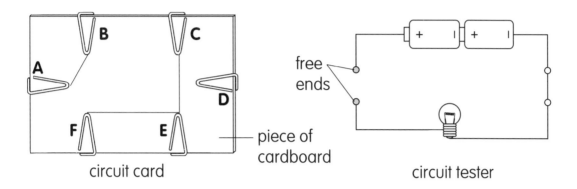

circuit card   circuit tester

Lee Lee connected the free ends of the circuit tester to different pairs of paper clips on the circuit card.

(a) Write 'Yes' or 'No' in the table to show what Lee Lee observed.

Paper clips connected to the circuit tester	Does the bulb light up?
A and B	
C and D	
E and F	
A and E	
B and F	

(b) For the bulb to light up, which two pairs of paper clips not stated in 6(a) could Lee Lee have connected to the circuit tester?

_____

7 Complete the crossword puzzle with the clues given.

Across

1. The tip of a bulb which is connected to the circuit is made of

   _____ .

2. The bulb is an artificial _____ of light.
3. The form of energy a bulb needs in order to work

Down

4. A bulb blows when too much _____ flows through it.

5. Very little _____ is contained in the space enclosed by a bulb.

6. The part of a bulb that gives out light and heat

systems

8 Study the actual circuits shown below.

(a)

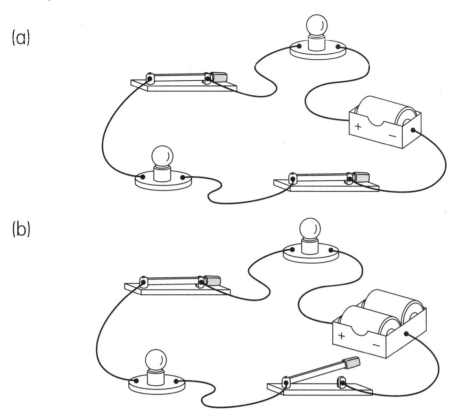

(b)

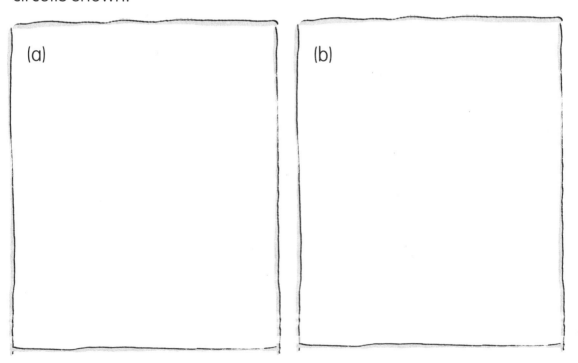

Draw circuit diagrams in the space provided to represent the actual circuits shown.

(a)

(b)

9 Study the circuits shown below. In the boxes provided, write the letters representing the bulbs that would light up.

(a)

(b)

(c)

(d)

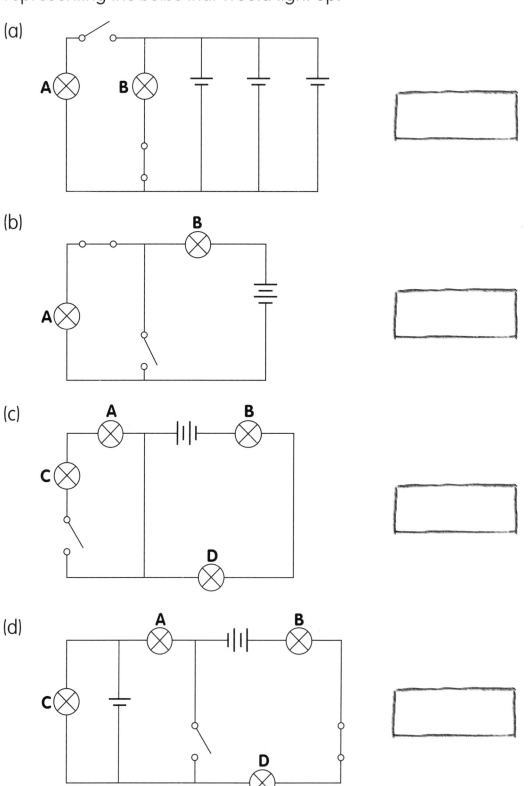

10 Study the circuits shown below. '⏻' represents a buzzer connected to the circuit. An observation can be made for each circuit. In the box provided, write the letter that represents the observation for each circuit.

Observations:
A — hear the buzzer sound only
B — see the bulb light up only
C — hear the buzzer sound and see the bulb light up
D — the buzzer does not sound and the bulb remains unlit

(a)

(b)

(c)

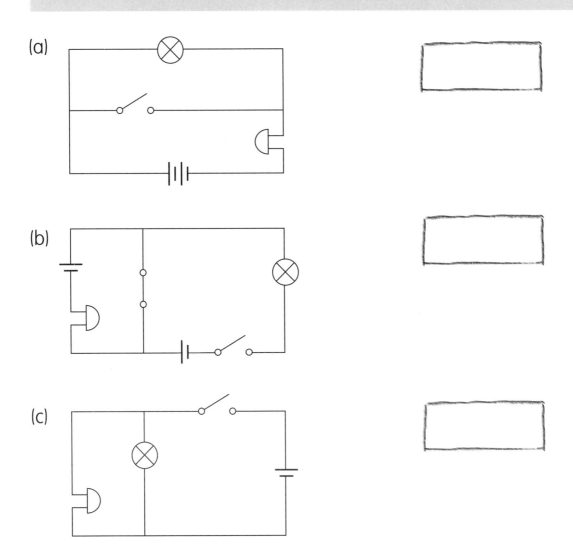

11 Sharom wanted to find out the number of batteries that would cause the bulb in a circuit to blow.

(a) Tick the box beside the method that Sharom should use to conduct his investigation.

☐ Method A

    Step 1 : Connect five batteries to a circuit.
    Step 2: Remove one battery from the circuit.
    Step 3: Observe whether the bulb lights up.
    Step 4: Repeat steps 2 and 3 until the bulb blows.

☐ Method B

    Step 1: Connect one battery to a circuit.
    Step 2: Observe whether the bulb lights up.
    Step 3: Add batteries to the circuit one by one until the bulb blows.

(b) Give a reason for the method you chose in 11(a).

_____

_____

_____

_____

(c) What variable would Sharom have to change during his investigation?

_____

(d) State two variables that Sharom should keep the same during his investigation.

_____

12 Vani changed the set-up of a circuit according to the steps shown below. She observed how the brightness of the bulb changed each time she set up the circuit differently. Her observations are also shown below.

Circuit	Observation
Step 1: 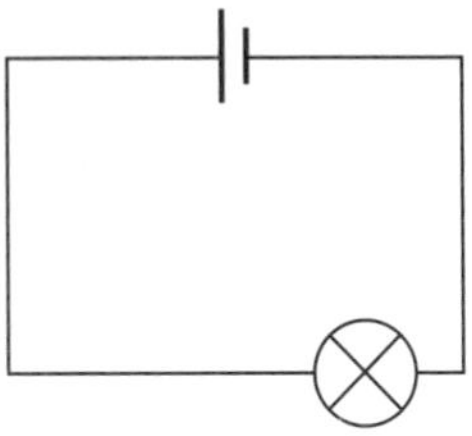	Bulb glowed
Step 2: 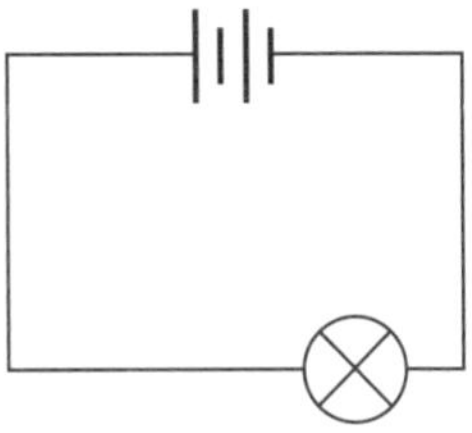	Bulb glowed brighter
Step 3: 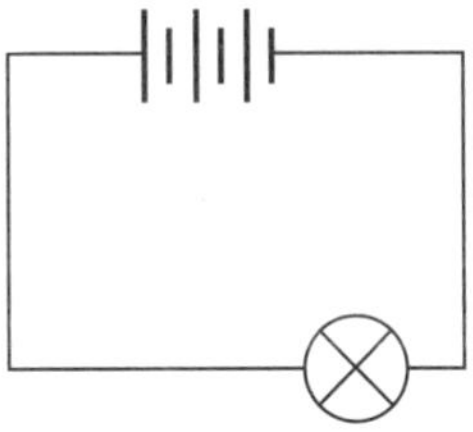	Bulb glowed even brighter
Step 4: 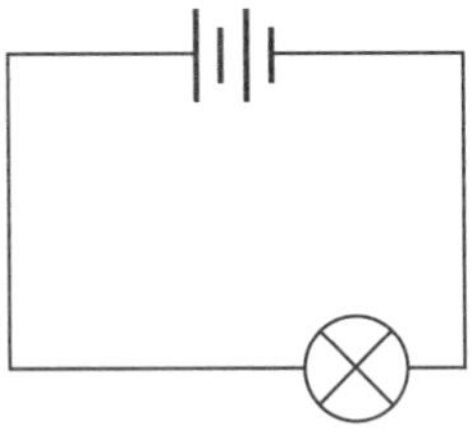	Bulb glowed less brightly
Step 5: 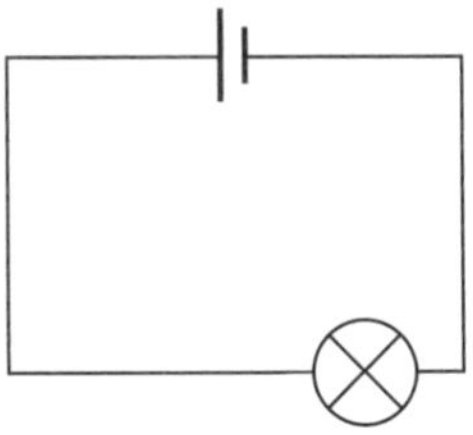	Bulb glowed even less brightly

(a) What do you think was the hypothesis for Vani's experiment?

_____

_____

(b) Explain why Vani's experiment was a fair test.

_____

_____

13 In an experiment, Wenda changed the set-up of a circuit according to the steps shown below and made some observations.

Circuit	Observation
Step 1: 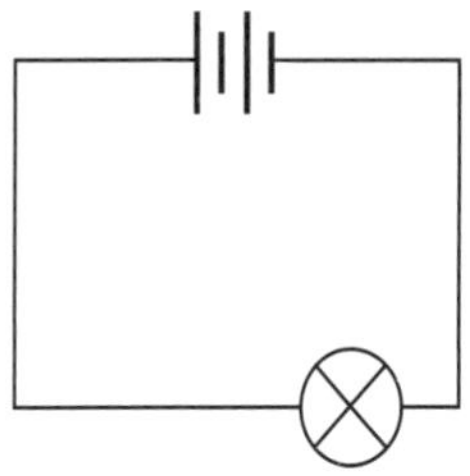	Bulb glowed brightly
Step 2: 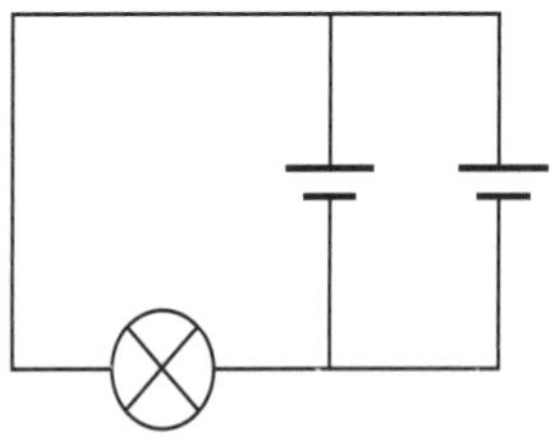	Bulb glowed less brightly

What do you think was the hypothesis for Wenda's experiment?

_____

_____

For each question, write your answer in the brackets provided.

1 An electric circuit is a path made up of electrical components through which _____ flows.
1) water
2) current
3) light
4) heat ( )

2 Each object shown in the diagram is described by a statement. Which statement is false?

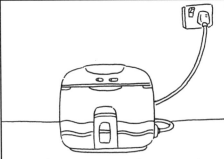

1) This rice cooker works by using electricity from the wall.

2) This torch is not an electrical system.

3) This watch needs electricity to work.

4) This sharpener does not need electricity to work.

( )

3 In which of the following circuits shown would the bulb light up?

A)

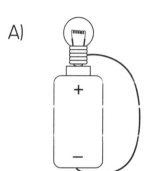

B)

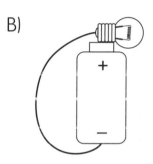

C)

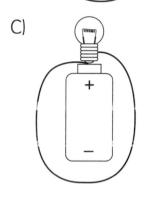

D)

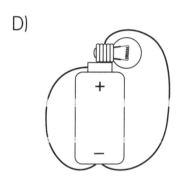

1) B only
2) A and B only
3) A, B and D only
4) B, C and D only   (   )

4 A battery has _____.
1) a North-seeking pole and a South-seeking pole
2) a plus pole and a minus pole
3) a like pole and an unlike pole
4) a positive pole and a negative pole   (   )

Refer to the following diagram to answer questions 5 and 6.

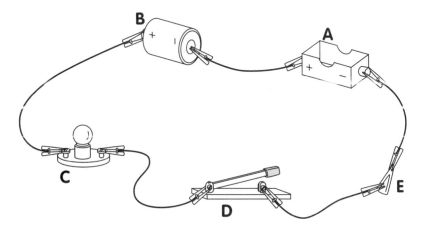

5 Which one of the components has a store of energy?
1) A
2) B
3) C
4) D
( )

6 Which of the following must you do to make the bulb light up?
A) Put a battery in battery holder A.
B) Close switch D.
C) Remove metal clip E from the circuit.

1) B only
2) A and B only
3) B and C only
4) A, B and C
( )

7 The shaded boxes in the diagram represent battery holders. Only bulbs P and R light up when batteries are put in _____.

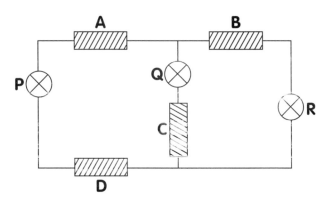

1) A and D only
2) B and C only
3) A, B and D only
4) A, C and D only
( )

8 In which one of the circuits shown would the bulb or bulbs glow least brightly?

1)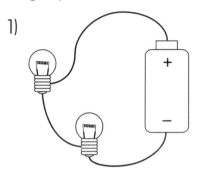

2)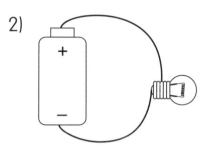

3)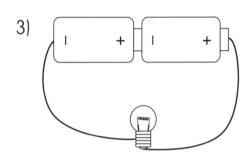

4)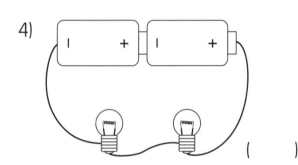

(   )

9 In which of the circuits shown would current flow?

A)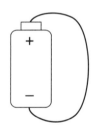

B)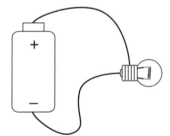

C)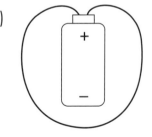

D)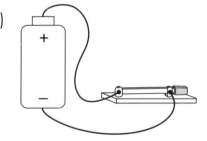

1) A and B only

2) B and D only

3) A, B and D only

4) A, B, C and D   (   )

Systems

10 Which of the following components can be used to close the circuit shown?

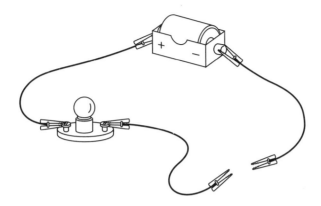

A) a battery
C) a closed switch

B) a battery holder
D) a bulb holder

1) A and C only
3) B, C and D only

2) A and D only
4) A, B, C and D   (   )

Refer to the following diagram to answer questions 11 and 12.

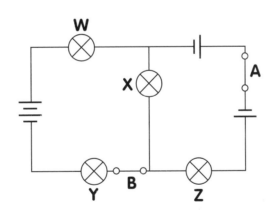

11 Which bulb or bulbs would remain lit when switch A is opened?
1) Z only
3) W and Y only

2) X and Z only
4) W, X and Y only   (   )

12 Which bulbs would remain lit when switch B is opened?
1) X and Z only
3) All of the bulbs

2) W and Z only
4) None of the bulbs   (   )

13 In the circuit shown, which switches should be left open and which switches should be closed so that only bulb X lights up?

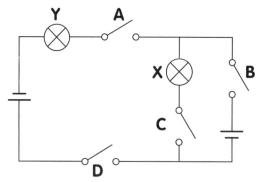

	Switch A	Switch B	Switch C	Switch D
1)	Open	Closed	Closed	Open
2)	Closed	Closed	Open	Closed
3)	Open	Open	Closed	Closed
4)	Closed	Closed	Open	Open

(   )

14 In the circuit shown, one closed switch must be opened and one opened switch must be closed so that only bulb X lights up. Which are these switches?

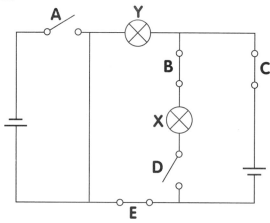

	To open switch	To close switch
1)	B	A
2)	B	D
3)	C	A
4)	E	D

(   )

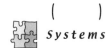

15 In the circuit shown, what is the least number of switches that must be closed for all the bulbs to light up?

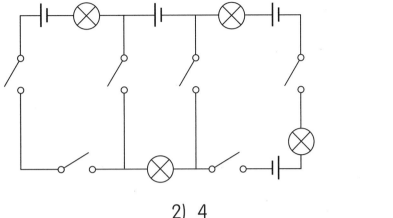

1) 3

3) 5

2) 4

4) 6

(   )

16 Which diagram shows a bulb that should not be lit?

1)

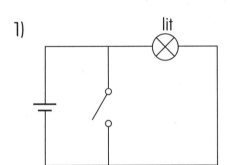

2)

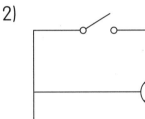

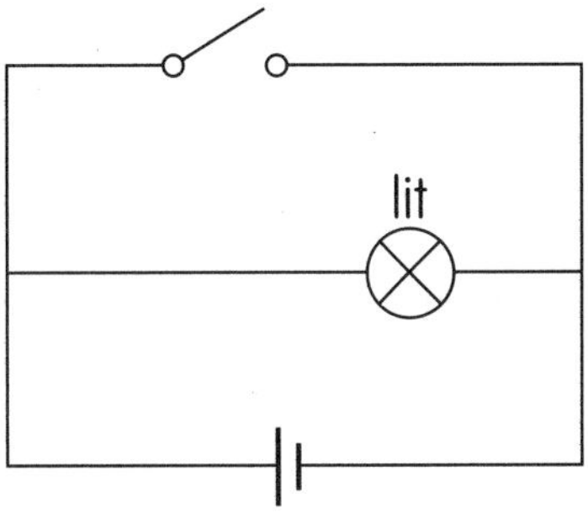

3)

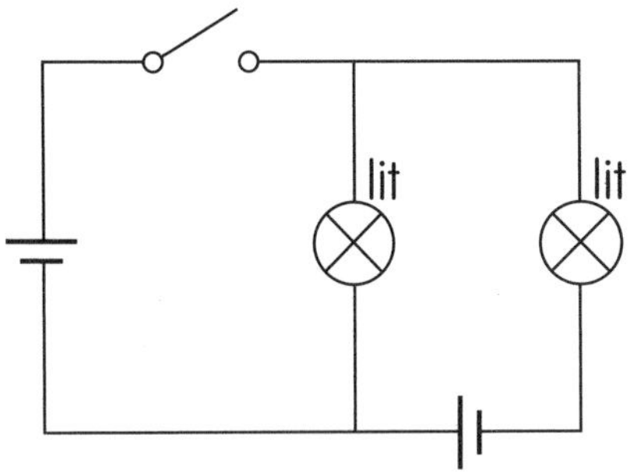

4)

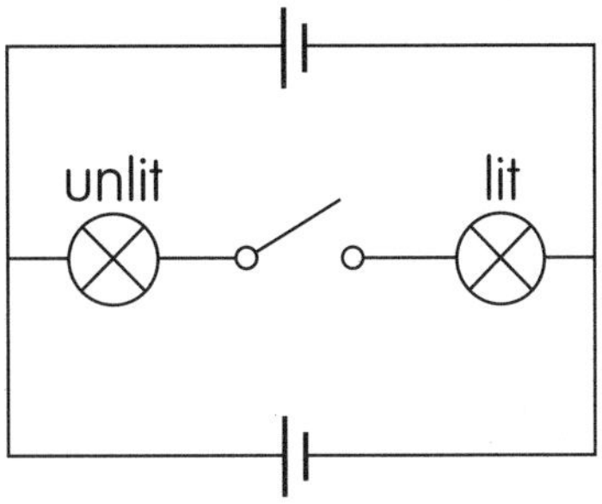

(   )

17 For a bulb to light up, both its metal casing and its metal tip must be connected to a circuit. Which diagram of the bulb explains why?

1)

2)

3)
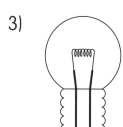

4)
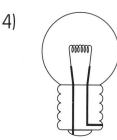

(   )

18 To ensure that the filament of a bulb does not break or melt easily, _____ .

A) it is completely enclosed in the bulb
B) oxygen is present in the bulb
C) the bulb must not be connected to too many batteries
D) it must be made of a metal that has a high melting point

1)   A and B only
2)   B and C only
3)   A, C and D only
4)   A, B, C and D

(   )

Systems

19 Study the actual circuit shown.

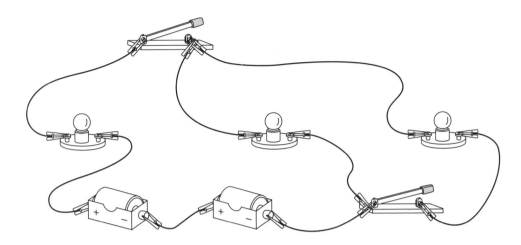

Which circuit diagram represents the actual circuit?

1)

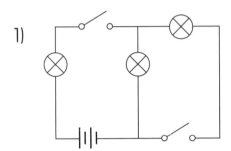

2)

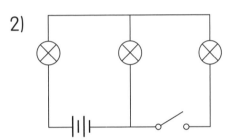

3)

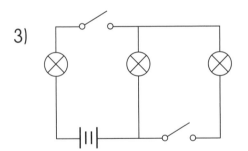

4)

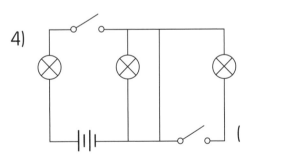

( )

20 Mohash conducted an experiment to find out how the brightness of the bulb would change when more batteries were connected to a circuit. The diagrams below show the steps of his experiment.

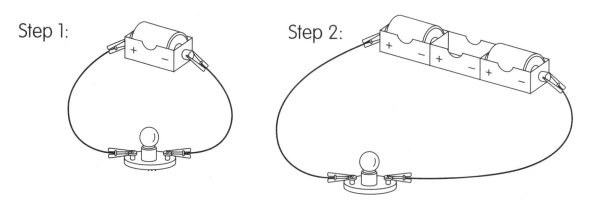

Step 1:   Step 2:

Which one of the following statements explains best why the bulb did not light up in Step 2?

1) The bulb blew when Mohash connected another battery to the circuit.
2) Mohash did not place a battery in the middle battery holder.
3) The battery holders were not connected to one another.
4) The circuit could not be closed as there was no switch connected to the circuit.   (   )

21 Which two circuits shown below can be used to compare how the arrangement of batteries affect the brightness of the bulb?

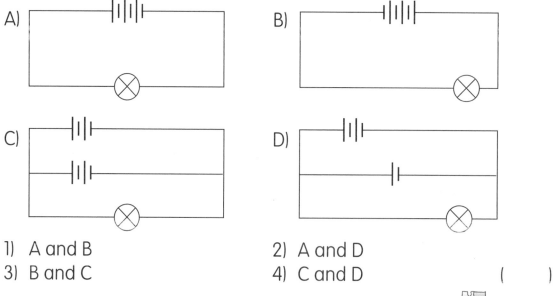

A)

B)

C)

D)

1) A and B
3) B and C
2) A and D
4) C and D   (   )

1 (a) Trace a path through the maze to lead 'Plug' to 'Socket'.
'Plug' cannot pass non-conductors of electricity.

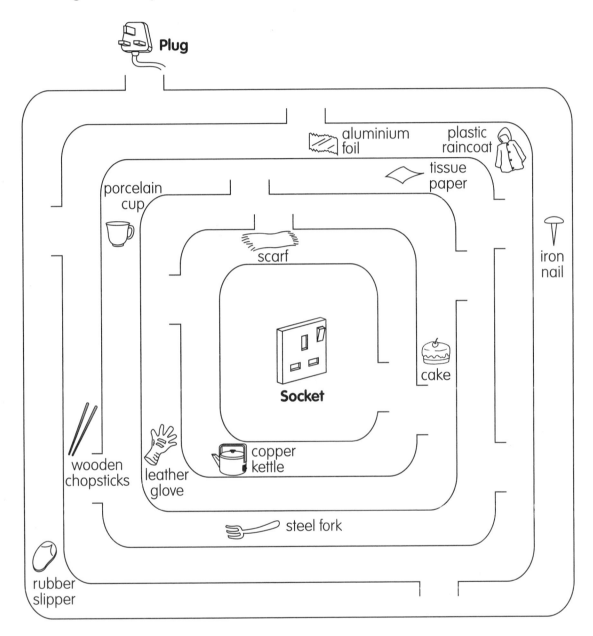

(b) In the table provided, classify the objects shown in the maze in 1(a).
Do not include 'Plug' and 'Socket' in your answer.

Conductors of electricity	Non-conductors of electricity
_____	_____
_____	_____
_____	_____
_____	_____
_____	_____
_____	_____
_____	_____
_____	_____
_____	_____

(c) What are non-conductors of electricity also called?

_____

2 For the bulb in Circuit A to light up, which object can be connected to the circuit where Box X is shown? Draw lines from the suitable objects to Box X.

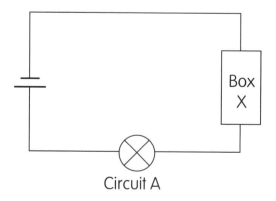

Circuit A

sewing needle

ping pong ball

chalk

iron pin

gold bracelet

 Systems

3 In the table below, tick suitable boxes to show the properties of each material.

Material	Properties			
	Conductor of		Insulator of	
	Electricity	Heat	Electricity	Heat
(a) copper				
(b) leather				
(c) aluminium				
(d) glass				

4 In the box beside each statement, write 'T' if the statement is true and 'F' if the statement is false.

(a) Metals are good conductors of electricity. ☐

(b) Metals are good conductors of heat. ☐

(c) Materials that allow electricity to pass through them also allow water to pass through them. ☐

(d) Electric current can flow through silver but not through gold. ☐

(e) A closed circuit is a continuous path of electrical conductors. ☐

(f) In a closed circuit, an electric current flows through the part of the switch made of plastic. ☐

5 Would the bulb in the circuits shown below light up when the switches are closed? Write 'Yes' or 'No' in the boxes provided.

(a)

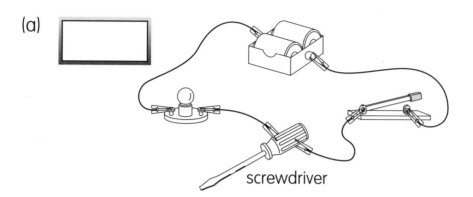

screwdriver

(b)

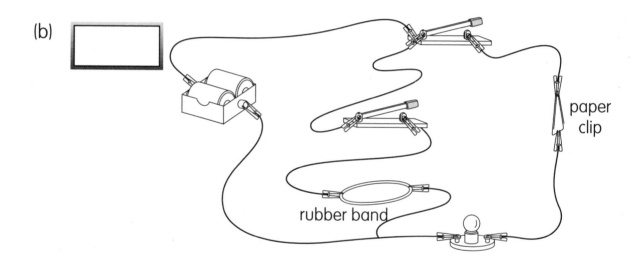

paper clip

rubber band

(c)

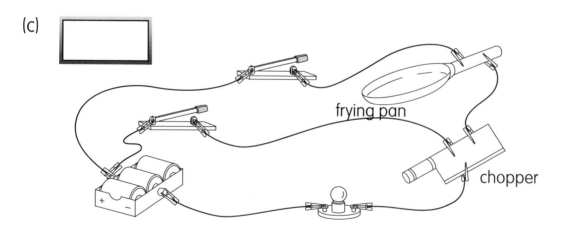

frying pan

chopper

6 Which parts of the picture show electricity not being used safely? Circle them.

7 The crossword puzzle was solved with the clues below. However, the clues were not numbered.

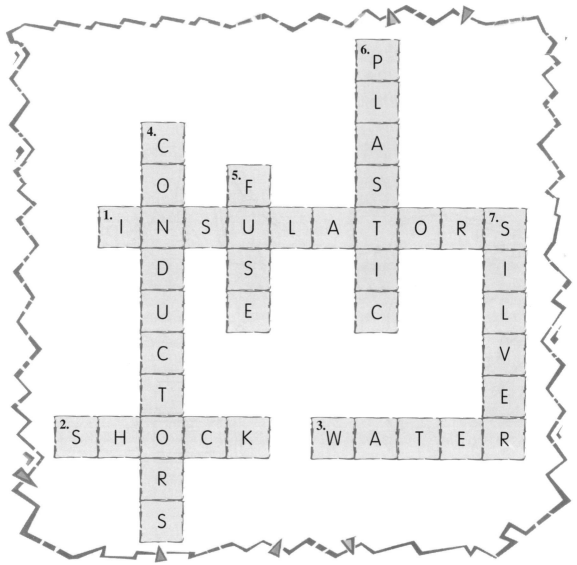

In the brackets provided, number the clues.

Across

(   ) A person may get an electric _____ if he does not use electricity safely.

(   ) A non-metal that conducts electricity

(   ) Materials that block an electric current from flowing through

(   ) An expensive metal that allows an electric current to flow through

(   ) The part of the plug that breaks a circuit when too much current flows through it

(   ) Materials that allow an electric current to flow through

(   ) Electrical wires are coated with _____ for the safer use of electricity.

8 Classify the following objects in the table provided.

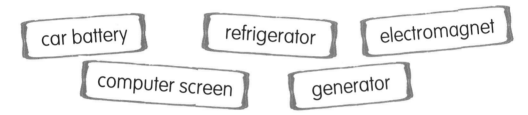

Produce electricity	Use electricity
_____	_____
_____	_____
_____	_____
_____	_____

9 Write a suitable caption to promote energy conservation for each picture.

(a) _____

_____

_____

_____

(b) _____

_____

_____

_____

(c) _____

_____

_____

_____

For each question, write your answer in the brackets provided.

1 Alan has the electric circuit shown below.

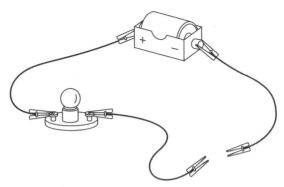

He connected a piece of wire to the circuit and the bulb lit up. Which one of the following diagrams show how Alan must have connected the piece of wire to the circuit?

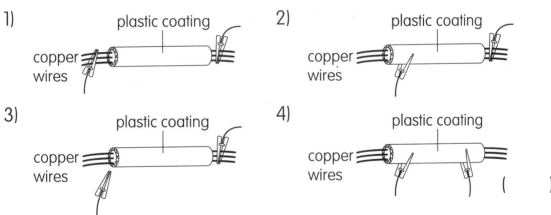

1) plastic coating
    copper wires

2) plastic coating
    copper wires

3) plastic coating
    copper wires

4) plastic coating
    copper wires

(   )

2 Which group of materials are conductors of electricity?
1) clay, glass and wood
2) aluminium, rubber and paper
3) copper, iron and silver
4) cotton, gold and plastic

(   )

3 Which one of the following statements is true?
1) All electrical insulators are metals.
2) Electrical wires can conduct electricity.
3) All conductors of electricity are made of iron.
4) Conductors of electricity produce electricity.

(   )

 Systems

4

```
                    Objects
```

Conductors of electricity	**Insulators of electricity**
copper coin	glass plate
steel paper clip	plastic knife
silver cup	aluminium foil
bamboo chopstick	cardboard box

Which of the objects above are classified wrongly?
1) copper coin and plastic knife
2) steel paper clip and glass plate
3) silver cup and cardboard box
4) bamboo chopstick and aluminium foil   (   )

5 In which of the following circuits would the bulb light up?

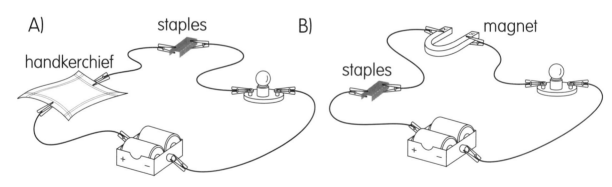

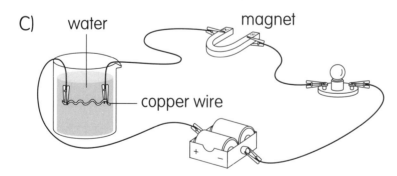

1) B only   2) A and B only
3) B and C only   4) A, B and C   (   )

Systems

6 Which bulbs should not light up in the circuit shown below?

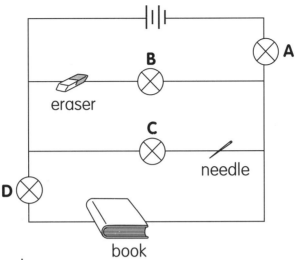

1) A and C only
2) B and D only
3) A, B and C only
4) A, B, C and D   (   )

7 In the diagram, SP, PQ, QR and RS represent thin wires made of different materials. The wires are connected at points P, Q, R and S.

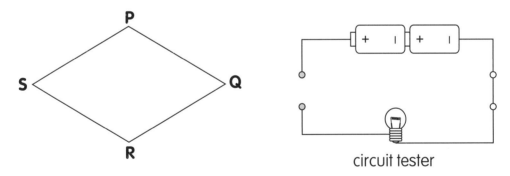

circuit tester

When a circuit tester is connected to points S and Q, the bulb lights up. When the circuit tester is connected to points Q and R, the bulb does not light up. Which one of the following statements must be true?

1) Wire SP conducts electricity.
2) Wire PQ does not conduct electricity.
3) Wire QR conducts electricity.
4) Wire RS does not conduct electricity.   (   )

8 Three pieces of electrical wire, each coated with plastic, were bundled together and put through plastic tubing. The ends of the wires were labelled A, B, C, D, E and F.

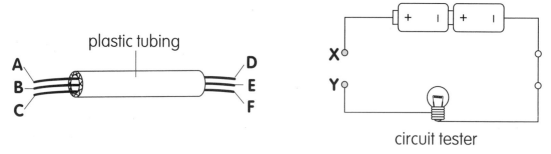

plastic tubing

circuit tester

The table shows whether the bulb of a circuit tester lit up when different pairs of wire ends were connected to the circuit tester.

		Wire end connected to the circuit tester at Y		
		D	E	F
Wire end connected to the circuit tester at X	A	No	No	Yes
	B	No	Yes	No
	C	Yes	No	No

Which one of the following diagrams show the correct arrangement of the wires underneath the plastic tubing?

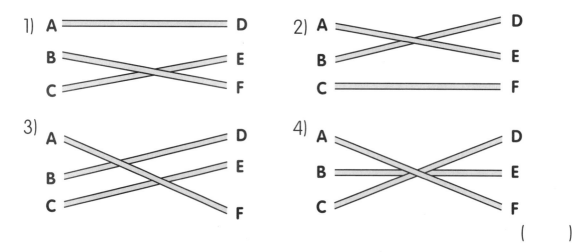

1) A — D, B — E, C — F

2) A — D, B — E, C — F

3) A — D, B — E, C — F

4) A — D, B — E, C — F

(   )

Systems

9 Four pupils made their own circuit testers. They connected different objects to their circuit testers to observe if the bulb lit up. Their observations are shown in the table below.

Pupil	Did the bulb light up for Object _____?		
	A	B	C
Nancy	No	Yes	No
Beng Hong	No	Yes	Yes
Zenda	Yes	Yes	Yes
Hanis	Yes	Yes	Yes

After studying the table, the pupils made the following statements.

Nancy   : Object B is a conductor.
Beng Hong : Object C is a non-conductor.
Zenda   : Objects A and C are non-conductors.
Hanis   : Objects A, B and C are conductors.

Who made a correct statement?
1) Zenda only
2) Nancy and Beng Hong only
3) Nancy and Hanis only
4) Beng Hong, Zenda and Hanis only   (   )

Worksheet 9
for Chapter 13

Forces

1 What type of force is needed to complete the following actions? Write 'push' or 'pull' in the boxes provided.

(a)

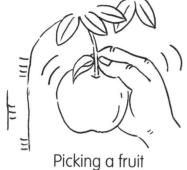

Picking a fruit

(b)

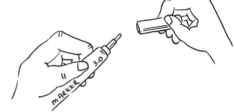

Replacing the cap of a marker

(c)

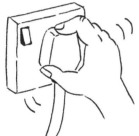

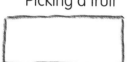

Removing an electrical plug from an electrical socket

(d)

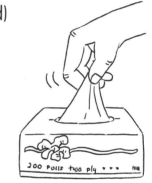

Taking a piece of tissue from a tissue box

(e)

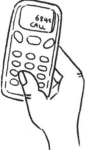

Dialling a friend's phone number

(f)

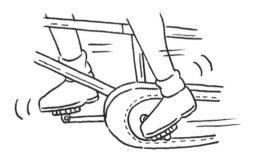

Pedalling a bicycle

2 A boy is kicking a ball home along the path shown in the diagram. Use the diagram to help you fill in the blanks below.

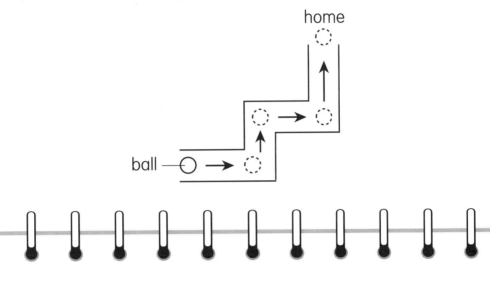

(a) For the boy to kick the ball home, the force applied on the ball must cause the ball to change _____.

(b) For the ball to move _____, a greater force must be applied on the ball in the direction that the ball is moving in.

(c) Another force is applied on the ball in the direction opposite to the moving ball. The ball may come to a _____.

3 In the space provided, write the letters A, B, C and D, starting with the action that uses the least force.

> **A** Pushing a pram with a baby inside

> **B** Pushing an empty supermarket trolley

> **C** Lifting a tree trunk with a crane

> **D** Lifting the lid of a kettle

Action that uses the least force ⟶ **Action that uses the greatest force**

4

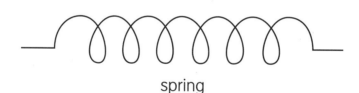

spring

To change the _____ of the spring shown, we can apply forces on the spring. The spring shortens if we _____ its ends towards each other. The spring lengthens if we _____ its ends in _____ directions.

5 A light wooden block was hung near a window. The diagrams represent photographs that were taken at the times stated.

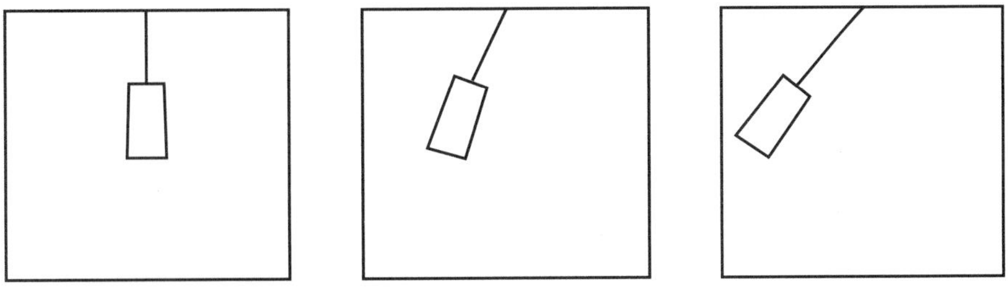

9.00 a.m.   10.00 a.m.   11.00 a.m.

(a) At what time was the wind blowing with the greatest force? How could you tell?

_____

_____

(b) State an example of how the force of wind can be
    (i) useful.

_____

_____

    (ii) harmful.

_____

_____

6 The following statements about forces are either true or false.
Tick the box under the correct heading.

	True	False
(a) A force cannot be seen.	☐	☐
(b) A force cannot be felt.	☐	☐
(c) A force is not matter.	☐	☐
(d) A force always causes things to move.	☐	☐
(e) A force can help us to do work.	☐	☐

For each question, write your answer in the brackets provided.

1 Which of the following actions use a pulling force?
   A) Removing white hair from the scalp
   B) Lifting a bag off the floor
   C) Fitting an electrical plug into an electrical socket
   D) Typing on a computer keyboard

   1) A and B only   2) A and C only
   3) C and D only   4) B, C and D only   (   )

2 A force cannot change the _____.
   1) direction of a moving object
   2) speed of a moving object
   3) mass of an object
   4) length of an object   (   )

3 Annan wants to roll the bowling ball to hit the bowling pins. In which one of the directions shown should he apply a force on the bowling ball?

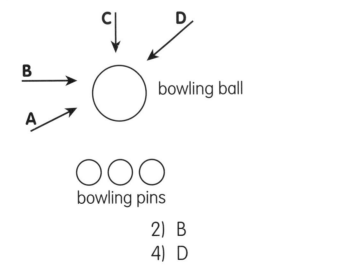

   1) A   2) B
   3) C   4) D   (   )

Refer to the experiment described below to answer questions 4 and 5.

Justin rolled balls of different masses down a slope. He wanted to find out how far a box would move when it was hit by the different balls. The diagram shows the set-up of his experiment.

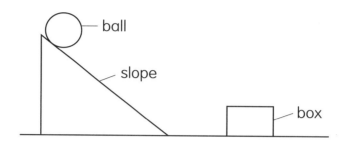

The following table shows the results of Justin's experiment.

Ball	A	B	C	D
Distance moved (cm)	68	35	75	50

4 Which ball hit the box with the second largest force?
   1) A
   2) B
   3) C
   4) D   (   )

5 To conduct a fair test, which one of the following variables did Justin keep constant?
   1) The mass of the ball
   2) The starting position of the ball
   3) The position where the ball comes to a stop
   4) The distance moved by the box   (   )

6 The following diagrams show that the force applied on the plunger caused _____ .

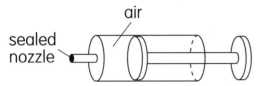

Before the plunger was pushed in

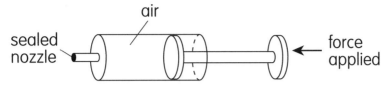

After the plunger was pushed in

1) the air in the syringe to disappear
2) the air in the syringe to change state
3) the mass of air in the syringe to decrease
4) the volume of air in the syringe to decrease   ( )

7 Four pupils were each given the syringe shown. They were told to push the plunger in lightly.

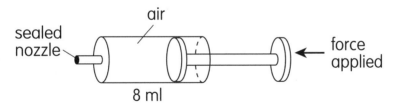

8 ml

Which one of the following diagrams shows the syringe after the plunger was pushed in with the greatest force?

1)
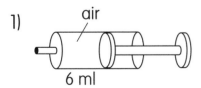
6 ml

2)
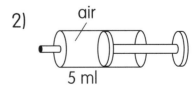
5 ml

3)
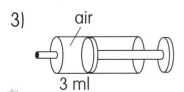
3 ml

4)
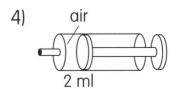
2 ml   ( )

8

The potter shown above is using force to change the _____
of the piece of clay.

1) colour
2) mass
3) position
4) shape   (   )

1 In a competition, the person who removed twenty nails from a wooden board in the shortest time was judged the strongest person. Three persons took part in the competition and used the hammers given to them, as shown in the pictures below. The nails were stuck equally tightly in each wooden board.

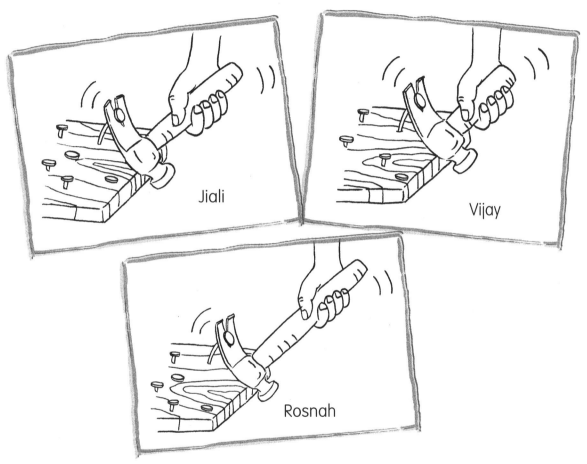

Jiali

Vijay

Rosnah

(a) Was this a fair competition? Explain your answer.

_____

_____

(b) What type of simple machine were the competitors using?

_____

(c) Who removed each nail

    (i) using the greatest effort? Explain your answer.

_____

_____

_____

_____

    (ii) using the least effort? Explain your answer.

_____

_____

_____

_____

(d) The competitors took the same amount of time to remove all twenty nails. Write the names of the competitors from the strongest to the weakest in the space provided.

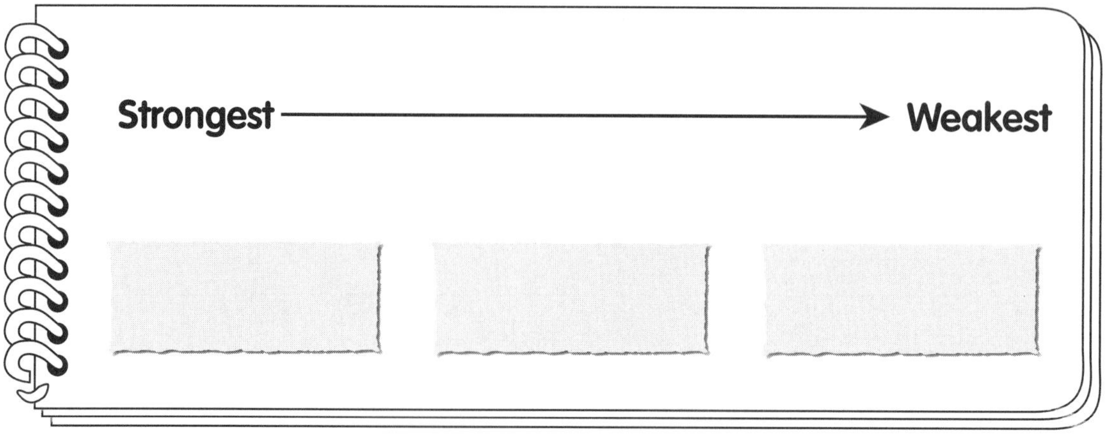

Strongest ————————————————➤ **Weakest**

2 Brema and Nassim each applied an effort on the lever shown in the diagram to lift a load.

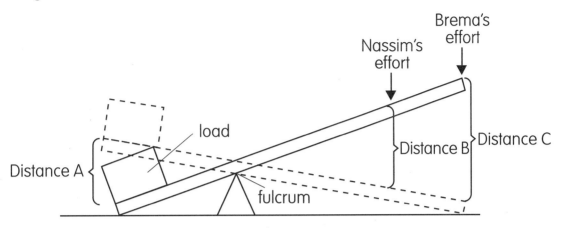

(a) (i) Distance A represents _____.

(ii) Distance B represents _____.

(iii) Distance C represents _____.

(b) Who applied a smaller effort to lift the load? Explain how you can tell by comparing Distance B and Distance C.

_____

_____

_____

_____

(c) Fill in the blank to complete the following sentence.

A greater effort is needed to lift the load when the effort is applied

nearer the _____ of the lever.

3 Some students carried out an experiment with the lever shown in the diagram. They applied an effort at End B to balance the load at End A. The effort needed was obtained by placing weights at End B and recording the mass of the weights used.

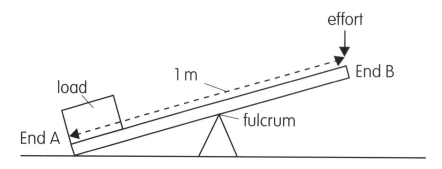

The experiment was repeated using the set-ups shown in the table below. Study the table and answer the following questions.

Set-up of the experiment	Load (g)	Effort (g)
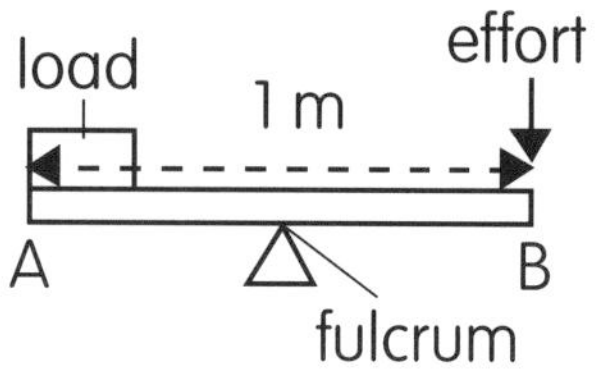 load, 1 m, effort, A, fulcrum, B	200	200
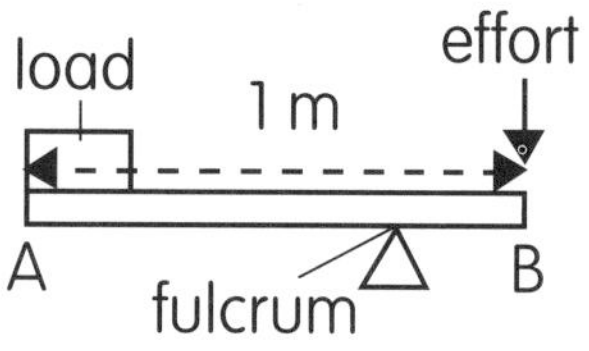 load, 1 m, effort, A, fulcrum, B	200	400
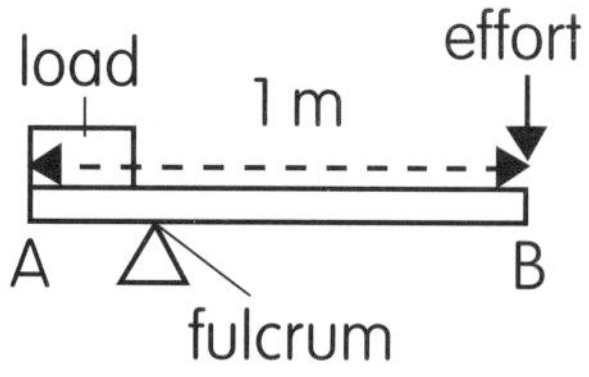 load, 1 m, effort, A, fulcrum, B	200	100

(a) What variable was changed in the experiment?

_____

(b) State two variables that were kept constant in the experiment.

_____

(c) From their results, what can the students conclude about the relationship between the effort needed to balance the load and the distance between the fulcrum and the load?

_____

_____

4 On each of the following diagrams, label the positions of the effort, the fulcrum and the load.

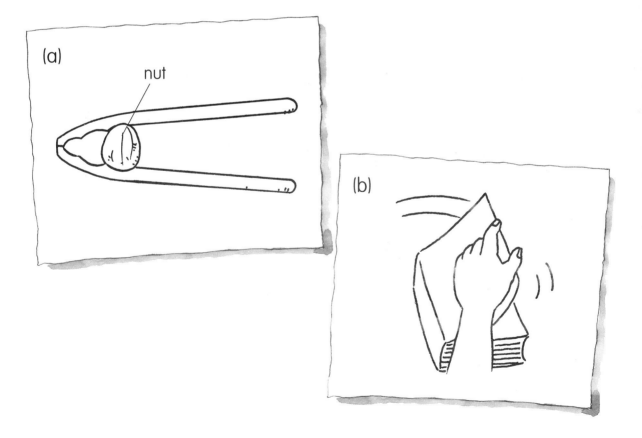

(a)

nut

(b)

5 Raj is using his arm as a lever as shown below.

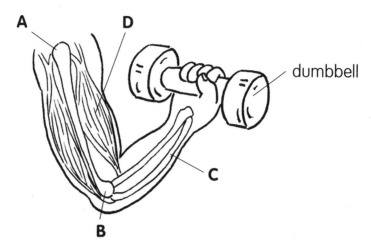

(a) What is the load shown in the diagram?

_____

(b) Which part of the arm, A, B, C or D in the diagram
   (i)   provides the effort needed to lift the load?

   _____

   (ii) acts as the fulcrum when the load is being lifted?

   _____

(c) Compare the direction of the movement of the effort and the load.

_____

6 (a) Name the type of pulleys shown below. Write your answers in the spaces provided.

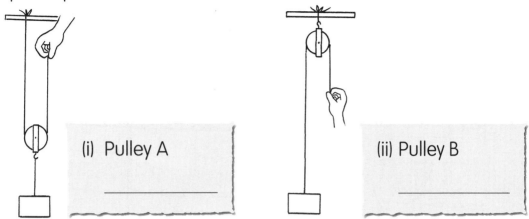

(i) Pulley A

_____

(ii) Pulley B

_____

(b) Compare the two pulleys for lifting the same load. Write your answers in the graphic organiser provided.

Pulley A	How different with regard to the	Pulley B
(i) _____ _____	movement of the pulley with the load?	(i) _____ _____
(ii) _____ _____	effort needed to lift the load?	(ii) _____ _____
(iii) _____ _____	direction of movement of the effort and the load?	(iii) _____ _____
(iv) _____ _____	distance moved by the load and the effort?	(iv) _____ _____

7 Hasni and Gerard had to pull their boats over the same distance for the boats to reach the coastline, as shown below.

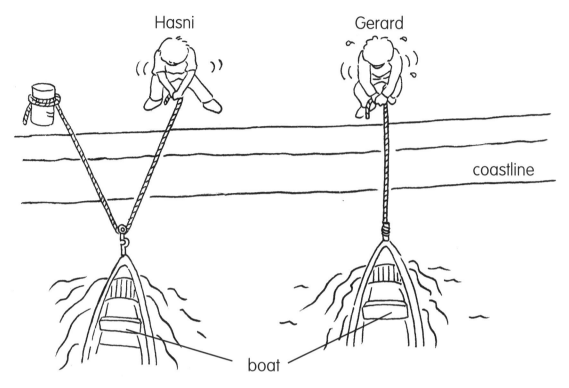

(a) What kind of pulley did Hasni use?

_____

(b) Write 'shorter than,' 'equal to' or 'greater than' in the blanks provided.

The distance moved by the boat to reach the coastline was	(i) For Hasni _____ (ii) For Gerard _____	the length of the rope he pulled in to move his boat to the coastline.

(c) _____ pulled his boat to the coastline with less effort.

 *Interactions*

8 Look at the pulley system shown in the diagram.

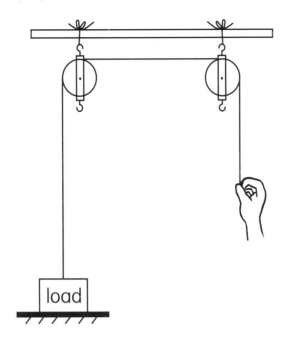

The following statements describe the pulley system shown above. In the boxes provided, write 'T' beside statements that are true and 'F' beside statements that are false.

(a) There are two pulleys in the system.

(b) One of the pulleys is a movable pulley.

(c) The effort needed to lift the load is reduced.

(d) For the load to be moved 1 m upwards, the effort would have to move 2 m downwards.

(e) The effort and the load move in opposite directions.

For each question, write your answer in the brackets provided.

1 Objects P and Q had the same mass. They were placed on the lever shown in the diagram. Object Q was shifted away from the fulcrum slowly. The lever would start to lift Object P when Object Q is moved to _____.

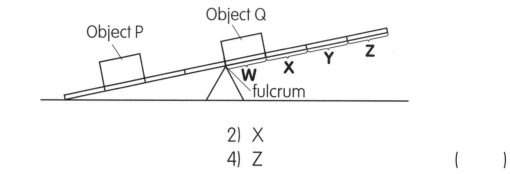

1) W	2) X
3) Y	4) Z

(   )

2 Study the lever shown in the diagram.

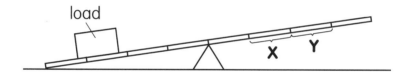

For the lever to lift the load, an object placed at _____.
1) X must weigh more than the load
2) X must weigh less than the load
3) Y must weigh less than the load
4) Y must weigh the same as the load

(   )

3 Four nuts, A, B, C and D, had the same size but different hardness. The same effort was needed to crack each nut with a nutcracker. However, the effort was applied at a different position for each nut. This is shown in the following diagram.

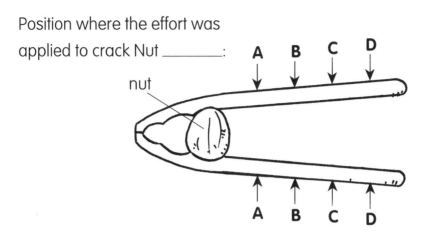

Position where the effort was applied to crack Nut _____:

Which one of the following statements is false?
1) Nut A is not as hard as Nut B.
2) Nut C is not as hard as Nut B.
3) Nut C is harder than Nut A.
4) Nut D is the hardest.   (   )

4 The diagram shows how Jierui uses a knife to cut an orange on a cutting board. The fulcrum of the simple machine is at _____.

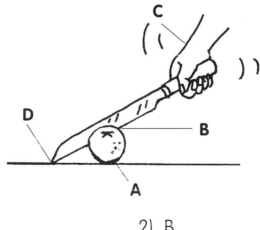

1) A	2) B
3) C	4) D ( )

5 To pick up an ice cube, effort can be applied on the pair of tongs at positions A, B or C, as shown in the diagram.

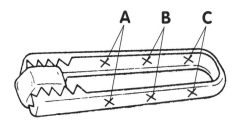

The effort needed _____.
1) is smaller when it is applied at A than when it is applied at B
2) is greater when it is applied at B than when it is applied at C
3) is greatest when it is applied at B
4) is smallest when it is applied at C   (   )

6 To reduce the effort needed to lift a load with a lever, the _____.
A) fulcrum should be moved as close to the load as possible.
B) fulcrum should be moved as far from the load as possible.
C) effort should be applied as close to the fulcrum as possible.
D) effort should be applied as far from the fulcrum as possible.

1) A and B only   2) A and D only
3) B and C only   4) B and D only   (   )

7 Which one of the following levers works differently from the others?

1)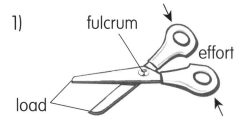

2)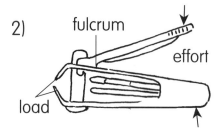

3)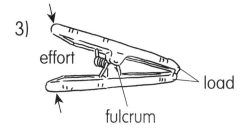

4)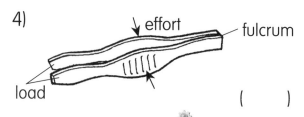

(   )

8 Study the graph to answer this question.

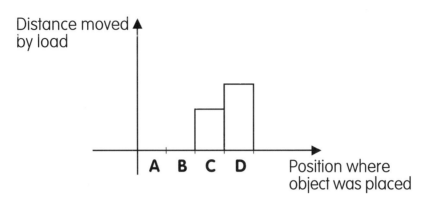

A load was placed on a lever. An object which weighed the same as the load was then placed on the lever at positions A, B, C and D. Which diagram shows where the load was placed on the lever?

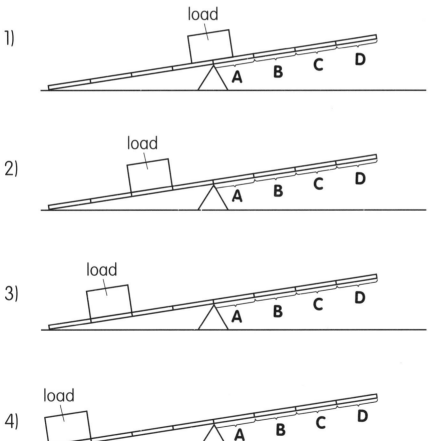

1)

2)

3)

4)

(   )

9 Yacob conducted an experiment with a lever by changing the position of the fulcrum. A diagram of the lever and his table of results are shown below.

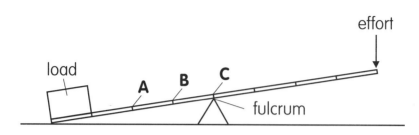

Position of fulcrum	Distance moved by load (cm)	Distance moved by effort (cm)
A	45	75
B	50	65
C	55	55

Which one of the following statements does not describe Yacob's observations?

1) The further the fulcrum is from the effort, the greater the distance moved by the effort.
2) The nearer the fulcrum is to the load, the smaller the distance moved by the load.
3) When the fulcrum is the same distance away from the load and the effort, the distance moved by the load and the effort are the same.
4) When the fulcrum is nearer the load, the distance moved by the load is greater than the distance moved by the effort.   (   )

10 Each diagram shows the position where the child applies an effort on a nail cutter to cut his or her fingernails. Who needs to apply the least effort?

1) Surin

2) Nisha

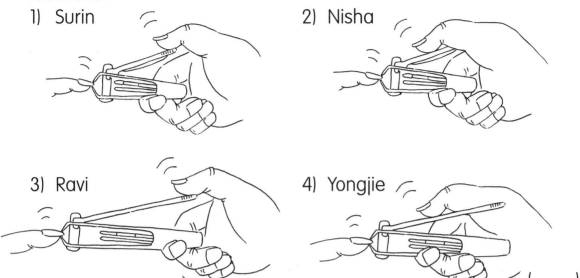

3) Ravi

4) Yongjie

(   )

11 Look at the diagram of the pulley below.

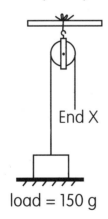

End X

load = 150 g

Which one of the following weights would cause the load to move upwards when the weight is tied to End X?

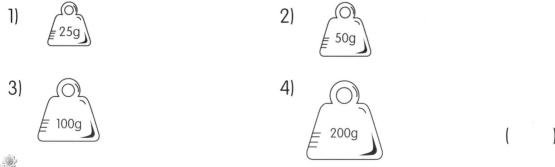

1)   25g

2)   50g

3)   100g

4)   200g

(   )

12 Study the pulley systems shown.

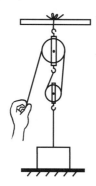 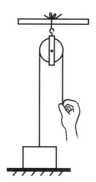

Which of the following statements about both machines are true?
A) Both contain a fixed pulley.
B) The effort and the load move in opposite directions for both machines.
C) The effort needed to lift the same load are the same for both machines.
D) The effort moves over a greater distance than the load for both machines.

1) A and B only   2) A and C only
3) B, C and D only   4) A, B, C and D   (   )

13 In which one of the following diagrams did the man apply the most effort to lift the load?

1)
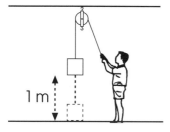
1 m

2)
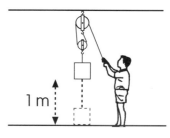
1 m

3)
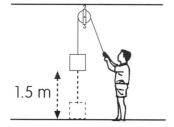
1.5 m

4)
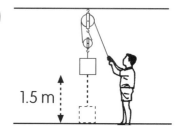
1.5 m   (   )

14 The effort moves over a greater distance than the load in a
_____ .

    A) fixed pulley

    B) movable pulley

    C) system of fixed and movable pulleys

    1) A only   2) A and B only

    3) B and C only   4) A, B and C   (   )

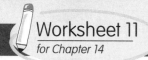
1 Cross out the machines that do not function as a wheel and axle.

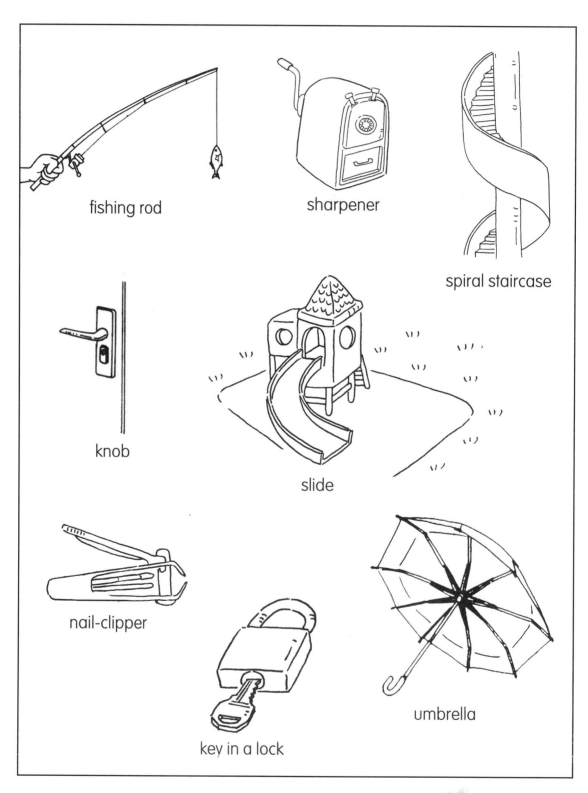

fishing rod

sharpener

spiral staircase

knob

slide

nail-clipper

key in a lock

umbrella

2 Arrange the machines A, B and C, according to the force that was needed to lift the load. Write your answers in the boxes provided.

(a)

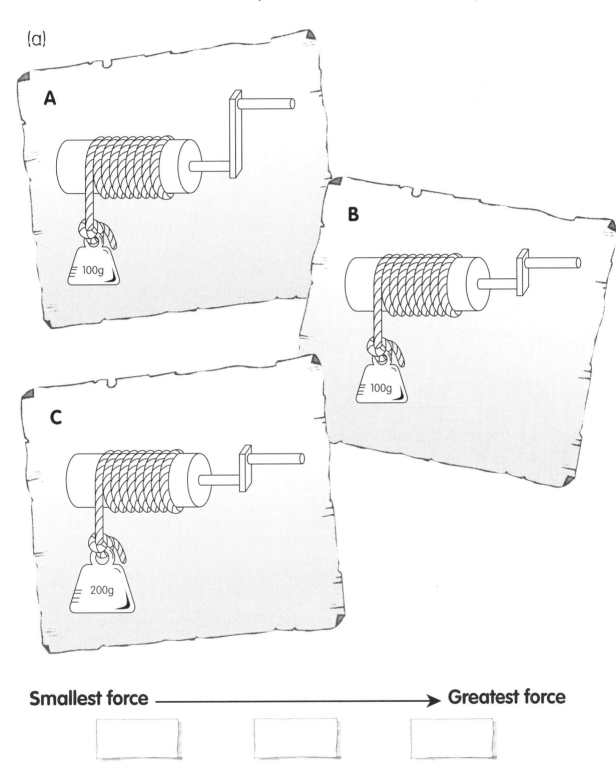

Smallest force ——————————————→ **Greatest force**

(b)

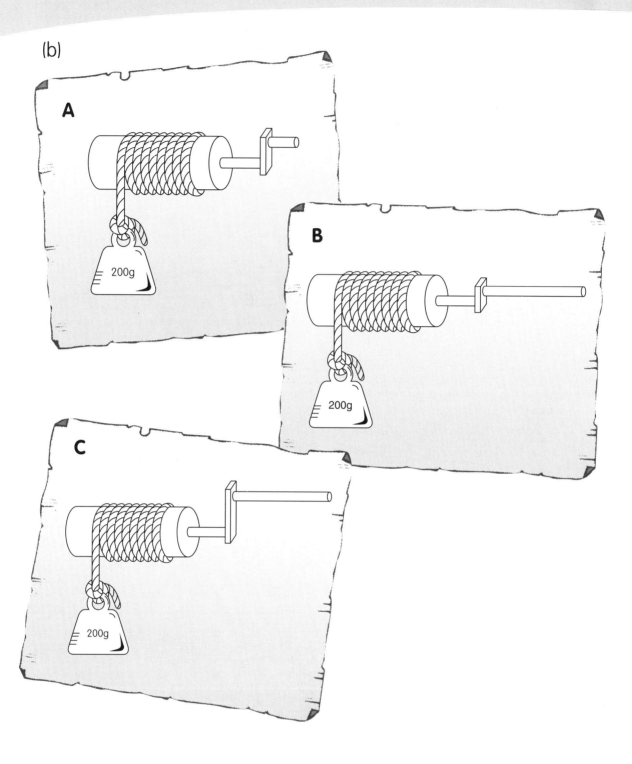

Smallest force ——————————————→ **Greatest force**

(c)

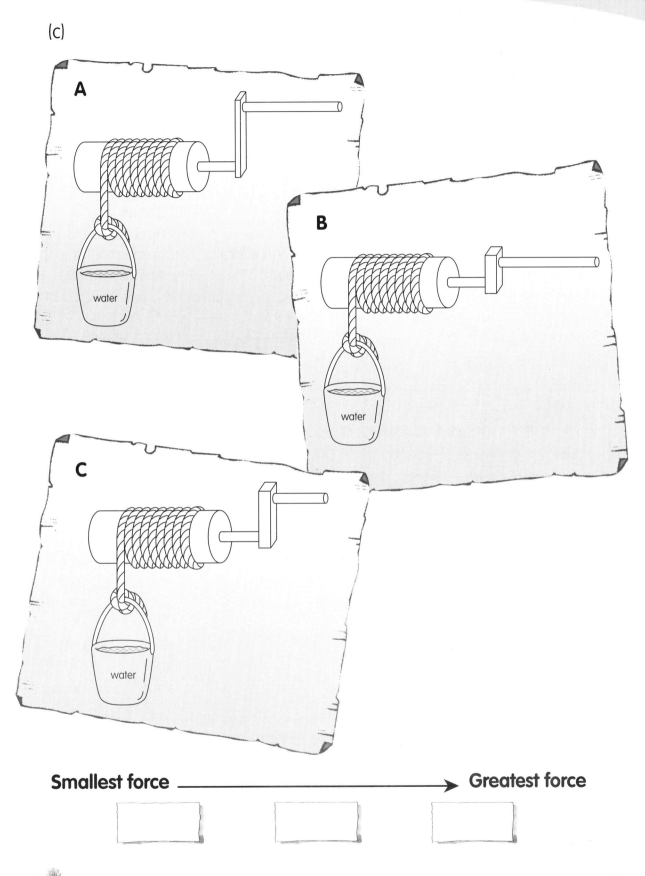

Smallest force ──────────────► **Greatest force**

3 In a competition, competitors have to fix a wheel to an axle to build a machine for lifting loads. The competitors are given axles of the same size but have wheels of different sizes to choose from. The person who uses his or her machine to lift the heaviest load is the winner. The diagrams below show the sizes of the wheel they picked.

(a) **Round 1**

Jiawei
applied twice the amount of force that Azman applied

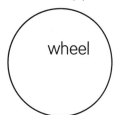

Azman
applied half the amount of force that Jiawei applied

Shanti
applied half the amount of force that Azman applied

The winner of this round is _____.

(b) **Round 2**

Viknesh
applied the same amount of force that Suzie applied

Suzie
applied half the amount of force that Shufen applied

Shufen
applied twice the amount of force that Viknesh applied

The winner of this round is _____.

(c) The competitors who lifted the lightest load in Rounds 1 and 2 will compete for a consolation prize. Who are they?

_____

4 Two men, Thiru and Zhihui, pushed a heavy wheelbarrow to reach a platform above the ground. They used different ramps to do so, as shown in the diagram.

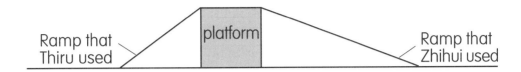

The two men started going up the ramps at the same time and they reached the platform together.

(a) Who was moving up the ramp faster?

_____

(b) Which man used a greater effort to push the load up the ramp?

_____

5 An elderly couple had to make their own ramps to get up a platform by the sea. They could choose from two planks, A and B as shown below, to make their ramps with.

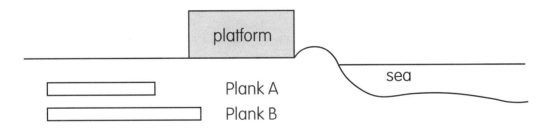

(a) The old lady chose Plank B. What could be the reason for her choice?

_____

_____

(b) The old man chose Plank A. What could be the reason for his choice?

_____

_____

6 Three children, Rahul, Mina and Yusheng, were riding on a special ferris wheel made up of three gear-like parts, A, B and C. The three parts fit together as shown in the diagram.

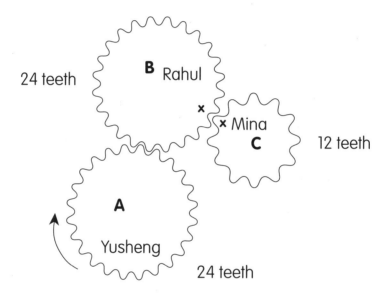

(a) If part A were turning in the direction shown in the diagram, what directions would parts B and C be turning in?

_____

_____

(b) At the start of the ride, Rahul and Mina sat facing each other. Their seating positions are marked '**x**' in the diagram. How many rounds would Rahul and Mina have each made on the ferris wheel before they faced each other again?

_____

_____

(c) Janice wants to ride in the part of the ferris wheel that moves faster. Where should she sit?

_____

For each question, write your answer in the brackets provided.

1 A set of wheel and axle is shown in the diagram. The handle should be fixed onto the wheel at _____ so that a load can be lifted with the least effort.

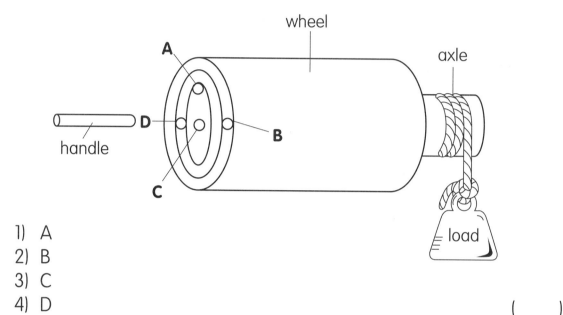

1) A
2) B
3) C
4) D

( )

2 In the diagram shown, the effort needed to loosen the nut is _____.

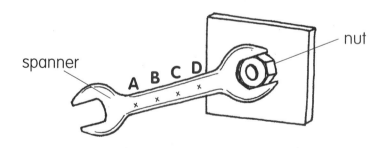

1) least when the effort is applied at D
2) greatest when the effort is applied at A
3) less when the effort is applied at A than when it is applied at B
4) greater when the effort is applied at B than when it is applied at C

( )

3 Which one of the following screwdrivers can be used to loosen a screw with the least effort?

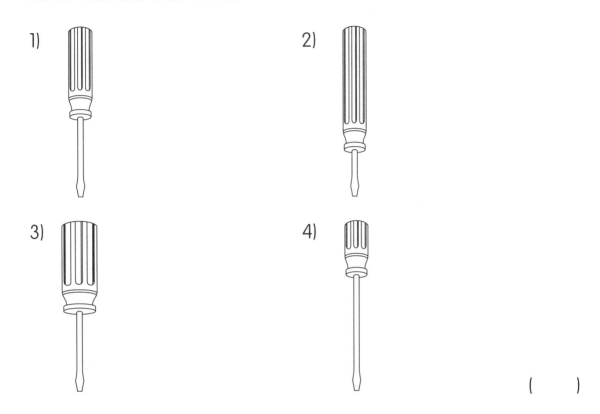

1)

2)

3)

4)

( )

4 An effort is applied to move a load from point A to point B up the ramps shown. For which ramp is the greatest effort needed?

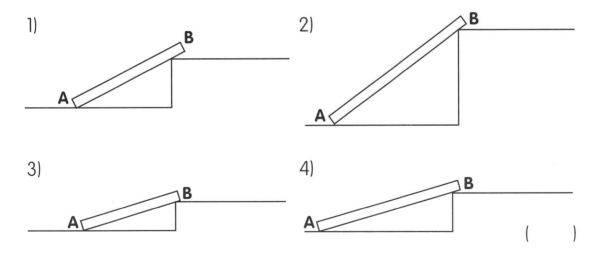

1)

2)

3)

4)

( )

5 The diagram shows the set-up of an experiment at the start. The number of bricks used was increased one at a time and the effort needed to move the load up the ramp was measured.

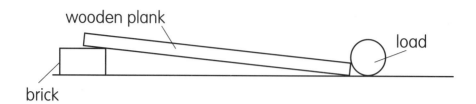

Which of the following would have been observed for the experiment?

A) The effort needed to move the load up the ramp increased as the number of bricks were increased.

B) The effort needed to move the load up the ramp decreased as the number of bricks were increased.

C) The distance moved by the load increased as the number of bricks were increased.

D) The distance moved by the load remained constant as the number of bricks were increased.

1) A and D only
2) B and C only
3) A, B and C only
4) B, C and D only   (   )

Refer to the diagram to answer questions 6 and 7.

6 The diagram shows a man moving a load up a van. What type of simple machine is the man using?
1) pulley   2) lever
3) gears   4) inclined plane   (   )

7 The simple machine shown in the diagram helps the man to move the load up the van with less effort. Which one of the following statements explains why?
1) It increases the distance from the effort to the fulcrum.
2) It allows the effort to move over a greater distance.
3) It allows the effort to move over a greater distance than the load.
4) It allows the effort and the load to move in opposite directions.
                                                                             (   )

8 Gears A, B, C and D are interlocked as shown in the diagram. Which gears move in the same direction when the gears are turning?

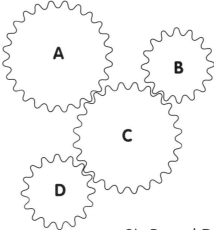

1) A and B only   2) B and D only
3) C and D only   4) A, B and D only   (   )

9 Gears X and Y are shown below.

16 teeth

Gear X

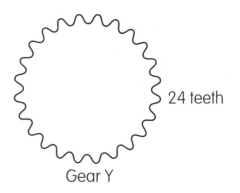

24 teeth

Gear Y

A gear is interlocked with both Gear X and Gear Y. It turns slower than Gear X but faster than Gear Y. Which one of the following diagrams show this gear?

1)  8 teeth

2)  16 teeth

3) 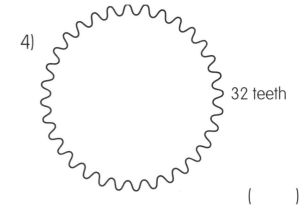 20 teeth

4) 32 teeth

( )

10 Which one of the following statements is always true for two gears that are interlocked?
1) They would turn in the same direction.
2) They would turn in opposite directions.
3) One gear would turn as fast as the other gear.
4) One gear would turn faster than the other gear.

( )